J 395.122 Ber
Berry, Joy Wilt.
May I? Please? Thank you!

4-97

D0578701

DATE DUE	Out	Due	In
MtseIll	8-31-00	9-30-00	

DEMCO

Weekly Reader Books presents

May I? Please? Thank You!

A Children's Book about Manners

by

Joy Wilt

Illustrated by Ernie Hergenroeder

Educational Products Division
Word, Incorporated
Waco, Texas

MONTROSE LIBRARY DISTRICT
434 SOUTH FIRST STREET
MONTROSE, COLORADO 81401

Author

JOY WILT is creator and director of Children's Ministries, an organization that provides resources "for people who care about children"—speakers, workshops, demonstrations, consulting services, and training institutes. A certified elementary school teacher, administrator, and early childhood specialist, Joy is also consultant to and professor in the master's degree program in children's ministries for Fuller Theological Seminary. Joy is a graduate of LaVerne College, LaVerne, California (B.A. in Biological Science), and Pacific Oaks College, Pasadena, California (M.A. in Human Development). She is author of three books, *Happily Ever After, An Uncomplicated Guide to Becoming a Superparent,* and *Taming the Big Bad Wolves,* as well as the popular *Can-Make-And-Do Books.* Joy's commitment "never to forget what it feels like to be a child" permeates the many innovative programs she has developed and her work as lecturer, consultant, writer, and—not least—mother of two children, Christopher and Lisa.

Artist

ERNIE HERGENROEDER is founder and owner of Hergie & Associates (a visual communications studio and advertising agency). With the establishment of this company in 1975, "Hergie" and his wife, Faith, settled in San Jose with their four children, Lynn, Kathy, Stephen, and Beth. Active in community and church affairs, Hergie is involved in presenting creative workshops for teachers, ministers, and others who wish to understand the techniques of communicating visually. He also lectures in high schools to encourage young artists toward a career in commercial art. Hergie serves as a consultant to organizations such as the Police Athletic League (PAL), Girl Scouts, and religious and secular corporations. His ultimate goal is to touch the hearts of kids (8 to 80) all over the world—visually!

This book is a presentation of Weekly Reader Books.
Weekly Reader Books offers book clubs for children from
preschool through junior high school.

For further information write to:
WEEKLY READER BOOKS
1250 Fairwood Ave.
Columbus, Ohio 43216

May I? Please? Thank You!

Copyright © 1979 by Joy Wilt. All rights reserved. Printed in the United States of America. No part of this book may be used or reproduced in any manner whatsoever without written permission, except in the case of brief quotations embodied in critical articles and reviews. This edition is published by arrangement with Educational Products Division, Word, Incorporated, 4800 West Waco Drive, Waco, Texas 76710.

ISBN: 0-8499-8137-9
Library of Congress Catalog Card Number: 79-50069
Bruce Johnson, Editor

8 9 / 89 88 87

Contents

Introduction   5

Part 1

Treating Other People with Kindness and Respect   13

   Meeting Other People for the First Time   14

   Meeting People Who Are Different   23

   Talking with Other People   31

   Eating with Other People   44

   Playing with Other People   60

   Working with Other People   69

   Helping Other People   80

   Saying Special Words and Doing Special Things
   for Other People   92

Part 2

Treating Other People's Possessions with Respect   103

   Treating Other People's Property with Respect   104

   Treating Other People's Things with Respect   118

Conclusion   125

Introduction

May I? Please? Thank You! is one of a series of books. The complete set is called *Ready-Set-Grow!*

May I? Please? Thank You! deals with manners and can be used by itself or as a part of a program that utilizes all of the *Ready-Set-Grow!* books.

May I? Please? Thank You! is specifically designed so that children can either read the book themselves or have it read to them. This can be done at home, church, or school. When reading to children, it is not necessary to complete the book at one sitting. Concern should be given to the attention span of the individual child and his or her comprehension of the subject matter.

May I? Please? Thank You! is designed to involve the child in the concepts that are being taught. This is done by simply and carefully explaining each concept and then asking questions that invite a response from the child. It is hoped that by answering the questions the child will personalize the concept and, thus, integrate it into his or her thinking.

May I? Please? Thank You! teaches that the basis of good manners is treating other people with kindness and respect. Rather than listing arbitrary rules of etiquette, the book refers to a basic, biblical guideline for relating to other people: "Do unto others as you would have them do unto you."

A series of vignettes presents fictional children in a variety of situations meeting other people for the first time; coming in contact with people who are different; talking, eating, playing, and working with other people; helping others; and saying special words or doing special things for others. After each little story, the reader is called on to think about how the Golden Rule applies to the situation, with questions about whether he or she has ever been treated in the way described, and if so, how he or she felt about it. Similar vignettes are used to teach about treating other people's possessions with respect.

May I? Please? Thank You! is designed to show children that their feelings about being treated kindly and respectfully are similar to anyone else's—and that everyone, no matter who he or she is or what his or her age, deserves to be treated with kindness and respect. Children may easily forget a set of unrelated rules for behavior, but the basic lesson of the Golden Rule, together with an ability to "put themselves in the other person's shoes," is all that's really necessary to develop good manners.

May I? Please? Thank You!

This book was written especially for you so that you could learn all about good manners. Do you know what it means for a person to have good manners?

A person who has good manners treats other people and their possessions with kindness and respect.

There is a special rule that all good manners come from. It is called the golden rule. It says . . .

Do unto others as you would have them do unto you.

The golden rule means that you should treat other people the way you want them to treat you.

Kindness and respect . . . that is what good manners are all about, and that is what this book is all about.

As you read, you will discover many ways that you can treat other people and their possessions with kindness and respect.

Part 1

Treating Other People with Kindness and Respect

MEETING OTHER PEOPLE FOR THE FIRST TIME

This is Frank. The people who know Frank often call him
"Cold Fish Frank." This is because . . .

when Cold Fish Frank meets a person for the first time, he won't tell him or her what his name is.

When Cold Fish Frank meets a person for the first time, he doesn't ask the person what his or her name is.

If someone wants to shake Cold Fish Frank's hand when they first meet, he just refuses.

Cold Fish Frank doesn't show an interest in the people he meets for the first time. He never encourages them to talk.

Have you ever met someone for the first time who . . .

> refused to tell you his or her name,
>
> forgot to ask you what your name is,
>
> failed to shake your hand even though you held it out for him or her to shake, or
>
> acted uninterested in you and didn't encourage you to talk?

How do you feel when a person does any of these things to you? Do you want to meet people who do these things?

Everyone likes to be treated with kindness and respect by a person he or she meets for the first time.

If you want to be treated with kindness and respect by a person you are meeting for the first time, you need to do everything you can to treat the other person with kindness and respect.

When you meet someone for the first time, remember to do these things.

Tell him or her what your name is.

Ask him or her what his or her name is.

Shake the person's hand if he or she holds it out for you to shake. (If you like, you can be the first to start a handshake by holding out your right hand.)

Be interested in the person and encourage him or her to talk.

MEETING PEOPLE WHO ARE DIFFERENT

This is Jude. The people who know Jude often call him "Rude Jude."
This is because . . .

When Rude Jude sees someone who is disabled, he stares at the person for a long time.

When Rude Jude sees someone of a different race or nationality, he points at the person and whispers about him or her.

When Rude Jude sees someone who looks or dresses differently than he does, he laughs and makes fun of the person.

When Rude Jude sees someone who is not as intelligent or skilled as he is, he does things to hurt the person and tries to get other people to do the same.

Has anyone ever stared at you?

Has anyone ever pointed at you and whispered about you?

Has anyone ever laughed and made fun of you?

Has anyone ever said unkind things to you?

Has anyone ever hurt you or gotten someone else to hurt you?

How do you feel when someone does any of these things to you?

What do you do?

If you want to be treated with kindness and respect, you must treat others with kindness and respect even though they may be different from you.

It is all right for you to be curious about people who are different from you. You may even be afraid of them or even want to avoid being around them. It will help if you ask questions to find out about people who are different from you.

If you want to ask questions about a person who is different from you, do it when the person is not around. Ask someone you trust, someone who will give you honest answers.

Hopefully you will find out that you can go directly to the person you are asking about and get more of your questions answered.

Remember. Treating someone who is different from you with kindness and respect means that you will try to do these things.

Try not to stare at the person for a long time.

Try not to point at the person and whisper about him or her.

Avoid laughing and making fun of him or her.

Never hurt him or her in any way.

Never get anyone else to hurt him or her.

This is Bill. The people who know Bill often call him "Butinski Bill." This is because . . .

When Butinski Bill is having a conversation with someone, he tries to do all of the talking. He will not talk about anything except himself and the things that interest him.

WELL, I'VE GOT THE BEST
LOOKING BIKE OF ANYONE
IN THE WHOLE CLASS... AND
BESIDES, I KNOW I'M BY
FAR THE BEST STUNT RIDER!
EVEN IF I DO SAY SO MYSELF!

Butinski Bill's favorite thing to do is to brag and boast about himself. So he does it all the time.

When someone is talking to Butinski Bill, Bill doesn't show any interest in the person. He doesn't look at the person, and he doesn't listen to what he or she is saying.

34

When someone is talking, Butinski Bill often interrupts. He doesn't care if the person has finished saying what he or she wanted to say.

Butinski Bill says whatever he wants to say whenever he wants to say it, even if what he says may hurt another person. Sometimes he says things just to be mean and hateful.

Butinski Bill will give a secret away, even though he has promised not to tell it to anyone.

Butinski Bill always talks loudly, even if he disturbs the people around him.

Have you ever tried to talk with someone who . . .

> wanted to do all the talking,
>
> wanted only to talk about himself or herself and what he or she is interested in,
>
> bragged about himself or herself all of the time,
>
> didn't show any interest in you or what you were saying,
>
> interrupted you in the middle of something you were saying,
>
> said things that hurt you,
>
> told a secret you asked him or her not to tell anyone, or
>
> talked in a loud voice?

How do you feel about talking with people who do these things? Do you enjoy having conversations with them?

No one likes to talk to a person who is not respectful and kind during a conversation.

If you want someone to be respectful and kind when that person talks to you, you must be respectful and kind when you talk to him or her.

Remember these things when you are talking with someone.

Try not to do all of the talking.

Try not to talk only about yourself and your interests.

Feel free to say good things about yourself, but avoid bragging and boasting all the time.

Show interest when a person talks to you. Look at the person and listen to what he or she is saying.

Try not to interrupt when a person is talking.

Allow the person to finish talking before you speak.
If for any reason you must interrupt someone, begin
by saying, "Excuse me."

Think before you say anything that might hurt another
person.

Try not to give away another person's secret.

Talk softly if there are people around who are bothered
by loud voices.

EATING WITH OTHER PEOPLE

This is Patsy. The people who know Patsy often call her "Patsy Pig." This is because . . .

when Patsy Pig has food, she eats it in front of other people even if they don't have any. Patsy Pig never shares her food because she wants it all for herself.

When Patsy Pig is eating a meal with other people, she doesn't care if they get any food. The minute Patsy Pig has gotten all of the food she wants, she starts eating. She never waits to see that everyone else has enough food before she begins.

If Patsy Pig wants something, she doesn't wait for it to be passed, and she doesn't think to ask anyone to pass it to her. Instead, she reaches across the table, in front of the people around her, to grab whatever she wants.

Patsy Pig often burps and hiccups at the table. Sometimes she even coughs or sneezes on the food.

Patsy Pig slurps her food, gets it all over herself, and makes a mess of the place around her by dropping and spilling food on the table and floor.

Patsy Pig stuffs food into her mouth until it is completely full, and then she begins to talk.

Patsy Pig talks all through the meal and never gives anyone else a chance to say anything.

MONTROSE LIBRARY DISTRICT
434 SOUTH FIRST STREET
MONTROSE, COLORADO 81401

51

When Patsy Pig has finished eating and talking, she interrupts the meal by leaving the table.

Patsy Pig never thanks the person who prepared the meal for her.

Has anyone ever eaten food in front of you when you didn't have anything to eat?

How did you feel? What did you do?

Have you ever eaten a meal with a person who didn't care if you got any food?

How did you feel? What did you do?

Have you ever eaten a meal with anyone who . . .

    reached in front of you to get what he or she wanted,

    burped, hiccuped, sneezed, or coughed on the food,

    slurped his or her food and made a mess of the place,

    stuffed his or her mouth with food and then talked,

    talked during the whole meal and never gave you a chance
    to say anything, or

    left you behind at the table when he or she was finished
    eating?

How do people who do these things make you feel? What do you
think about them?

Have you ever made something for someone who forgot to thank you?

How did it make you feel? Would you want to make something else
for that person?

No one likes to eat with anyone who is selfish and rude.

Everyone likes to be treated with kindness and respect when eating with other people.

If you want the people you eat with to be kind and respectful, you will need to make sure that you treat them with kindness and respect.

Remember these things when you eat with other people.

Try not to eat food in front of someone who doesn't have anything to eat.

Make sure everyone at the table has enough food before you begin eating your meal.

Kindly ask the people around you to pass things that are out of your reach.

Try not to burp or hiccup while you are eating. If you must sneeze or cough, cover your mouth and turn your head away from the food.

Try not to make a mess around you when you eat. To keep your clothes clean, spread a napkin on you lap to catch food that you accidentally drop.

Try not to stuff your mouth full of food.

Try not to talk when you have food in your mouth.

Try not to do all of the talking during a meal. Give someone else a chance to talk.

Ask to leave the table when you have finished eating and talking.

Remember to thank the person who was kind enough to prepare your food.

This is Mortimer. The people who know Mortimer often call him "Bad Sport Mort." This is because . . .

Bad Sport Mort always wants to decide what
and how everyone will play. If someone doesn't
do exactly what Bad Sport Mort wants, he won't play at all.

61

Winning is the most important thing to Bad Sport Mort, and he will often try to change the rules of the game just so that he can win.

Bad Sport Mort seldom follows the rules of the game—although he makes sure everyone else does. In fact, he often cheats in order to win.

Bad Sport Mort refuses to share his things with anyone.

HEY, MORT, I DON'T HAVE ANY MARBLES. MAY I BORROW A FEW OF YOURS?

TOUGH LUCK, KID! YOU'LL HAVE TO GET YOUR OWN MARBLES IF YOU WANT TO PLAY IN THIS GAME. I'M NOT LOANING MINE TO ANYONE!

If Bad Sport Mort loses, he gets angry, cries, screams, yells, and often throws things.

Have you ever played with someone who . . .

  wouldn't play unless you played exactly what and how he or she wanted you to play,

  changed the rules just so that he or she could win,

  seldom played by the rules, even though he or she insisted that you did,

  cheated to make sure that he or she won,

  refused to share his or her things with you, or

  got angry and threw a tantrum if he or she lost?

How do you feel when a person does these things? Do you enjoy playing with people who act this way?

No one likes to play with anyone who is demanding, selfish, and unfair. Everyone likes to be treated with kindness and respect when playing with other people.

If you want people to be kind and respectful when they play with you, you will need to make sure that you treat them with kindness and respect when you play with them.

When you play with someone else, remember these things.

Take turns with the people you are playing with deciding what and how you will play.

Decide on the rules of a game before the game begins. If everyone playing the game wants to change the rules during the game, then it is OK to do so.

Play by the rules.

Do not cheat.

Share your things whenever you can.

If you should lose, don't give up or stop trying. Remember that everyone loses once in a while and no one wins all of the time.

This is Jerry Jones. People who know Jerry Jones often call him "Lazybones Jones." This is because . . .

Lazybones Jones will put off doing his work for as long as he possibly can in hopes that he will not have to do it at all.

If Lazybones Jones is working with someone else, he will do everything he can to make sure that the other person does most of the work.

No matter what the job is or how much work there is to be done, Lazybones Jones always complains about it.

Lazybones Jones never does his work very well. Usually someone else has to do his work over again so that it will be done right.

Lazybones Jones seldom finishes his work. Instead, he leaves it for someone else to do.

Lazybones Jones always has a lot of excuses for why he didn't finish his work or do it well.

Have you ever worked with a person who . . .

> tried to put off doing his or her work for as long as he or she could in hopes of not having to do it at all,

> tried to make it so that you would do more work than he or she did,

> complained the entire time he or she was working,

> did not do a good job when he or she worked,

> seldom finished his or her work, or

> had a lot of excuses why his or her work was not finished or why it was not done well?

How do you feel about people who do these things? Do you want to work with them?

No one likes to work with a person who is lazy, unfair, and complaining.

I DON'T LIKE YOUR ATTITUDE!
I'M NOT GOING TO STAY HERE
AND LISTEN TO YOU GRIPE.
I'M GOING TO WEED SOMEWHERE
ELSE — AWAY FROM YOU!

Everyone likes to be treated with kindness and respect when working with other people.

If you want people to be kind and respectful when they work with you, you will need to make sure that you treat them with kindness and respect when you work with them.

When you work with someone else, remember these things.

Begin working as soon as you can. Don't put off the work in hopes that you won't have to do it at all.

Always do your fair share of the work. Don't make someone else have to do more work than you.

Don't complain while you work. No one likes to listen to someone else complain all the time.

Whatever you do, do your work well. No one should have to do your work over again.

Finish the work you start. It is not fair for you to leave your work for someone else to do.

HELPING OTHER PEOPLE

This is Hanna. The people who know Hanna often call
her "No Help Hanna." This is because . . .

when No Help Hanna is with someone who is carrying a heavy load, she never offers to help carry anything.

When No Help Hanna sees a person struggling with a door, she never offers to help open the door.

When No Help Hanna is sitting in a seat that someone else needs more than she does, she will not offer to give her seat to the person.

When No Help Hanna sees someone drop something, she won't pick it up for the person.

When No Help Hanna sees someone struggling with a piece of clothing, she doesn't offer to help the person.

When No Help Hanna is asked to get something by someone, she usually refuses.

If a person is upset or hurt, No Help Hanna never stops to help.

Have you ever carried a heavy load, and wished that someone would help carry it?

Have you ever tried to open a heavy door or tried to open a door while your arms were full, and wished that someone had been there to open it for you?

Have you ever needed to sit down somewhere, and wished that someone would share his or her seat with you?

Have you ever dropped something when your hands were full, and wished that someone would pick it up for you?

Have you ever wished someone would help you put your coat on or take it off?

Have you ever needed someone to get something for you?

Have you ever been upset and wished someone would help you feel better?

Have you ever gotten hurt and needed someone to help you?

No one likes to help someone who is not helpful.

Everyone likes to be treated with kindness and respect
when needing help.

If you want people to be kind and respectful when you need help, you will need to make sure that you treat them with kindness and respect when they need help.

If you want to be helpful, do these things when you have a chance.

Help someone carry his or her load.

Open a door for someone.

Offer someone your seat if he or she needs it more than you do.

When a person drops something, pick it up for him or her.

Help a person when he or she is struggling to put on a piece of clothing.

Help a person when he or she asks you to get something he or she needs.

Do what you can to help a person who is upset.

Do your best to help a person if he or she gets hurt.

SAYING SPECIAL WORDS AND DOING

SPECIAL THINGS FOR OTHER PEOPLE

There are special words that can help you express kindness and respect to other people. Here are some of them.

How are you today? Words to say when you care about how a person is doing.

Fine, thank you. How are you? Words to say when a person has asked you how you are. You should not say these words unless you really do feel fine.

May I? Words to say when you would like to do something.

<u>Please</u>. A word to say when you want something from someone else.

<u>Thank you</u>. Words to say when you appreciate what someone has done for you or when he or she has given you something.

<u>No, thank you</u>. Words to say when a person has offered you something you do not want.

<u>You're welcome</u>. Words to say when a person has thanked you for something you have given him or her.

<u>Excuse me</u>. Words to say when you have interrupted a person, bumped into someone, interfered with what someone was doing, or hurt a person's feelings.

<u>Pardon</u>? A word to say when you did not hear what someone has said and you want the person to repeat it.

<u>I'm sorry</u>. Words to say when you have done something wrong to someone else.

If you say these words honestly and sincerely, whenever and wherever you need to, you will probably make other people feel good, and they may in turn treat you with kindness and respect.

There are some special things that you can do to show kindness and respect to other people. Here are some of them.

Try to cover your mouth when you yawn, sneeze, or cough.

It is not fair for you to spread the germs in your mouth other people.

Be as quiet as you can around people who are sleeping, resting, talking to someone, thinking, watching TV, or listening to the radio or record player.

This is so you won't disturb them.

Try to be on time wherever you go. This way you won't make people wait for you.

Take turns with others being first, and don't always try to get the biggest and best for yourself.

If you meet a person who is walking directly toward you, step out of the way and let the other person pass.

Walk behind a person who is watching or doing something or talking with another person so that you will not interfere with what's going on.

Treating people with kindness and respect . . .

   no matter who they are,
   no matter where they are, and
   no matter when it is . . .

is what good manners are all about.

Part 2

Treating Other People's Possessions with Respect

This is Carrie. The people who know Carrie often call her "Careless Carrie." This is because . . .

Careless Carrie doesn't care about anyone else's property. Careless Carrie never puts her trash in a trash can. Instead, she drops it on the ground for someone else to pick up.

Careless Carrie writes or scratches on other people's property whenever she feels like it.

Careless Carrie abuses other people's property and doesn't care if she damages or destroys it.

Careless Carrie doesn't wipe her shoes off before she walks into someone's home, and she ends up bringing mud, water, and dirt in with her.

When visiting someone else's home, Careless Carrie snoops through every room, closet, and drawer. Careless Carrie touches everything in sight and doesn't care if she damages or destroys something.

Careless Carrie never has anything nice to say about anyone's home. Instead, she says things that hurt other people's feelings.

If Careless Carrie makes a mess at someone else's home, she never cleans it up. She never puts away other people's things after she is finished using them.

How do you feel when you see . . .

trash that someone has thrown on the ground,

writing that someone has scratched or written on walls, fences, or trees, or

property that someone has damaged or destroyed?   What do you think

Have you ever had a person visit you who . . .

> brought mud, water, or dirt in with him or her,
>
> snooped in the rooms, closets, and drawers,
>
> touched everything in sight, even if you didn't want him or her to,
>
> made a mess and left it for you to clean up,
>
> played with something and then left it for you to put away, or
>
> said unkind things about your home?

How do you feel about people who do these things? Do you enjoy having them visit you?

No one likes to be around a person who abuses other people's property.

Everyone likes to have his or her property treated with respec

If you want other people to respect your property, you will need to make sure that you respect their property.

Remember these things when you visit other people's property.

Put your trash in a trash can instead of throwing it on the ground.

Do not write on walls or any other place on public or private property.

Try not to misuse, damage, or destroy other people's property.

Wipe your feet off before you enter the place you are visiting so that you will not track mud, water, or dirt inside.

Go only into the places you have permission to go and only look in the closets and drawers you have permission to look in.

Ask permission to touch and handle those things you would like to play with.

If you make a mess, clean it up.

Put away the things you use when you are finished with them.

Don't say things about the place where you are visiting that might hurt someone's feelings.

This is Dan. People who know Dan often call him "Destructive Dan." This is because . . .

when Destructive Dan borrows something from another person, he doesn't return it.

When Destructive Dan uses another person's things, he often misuses, loses, damages, or sometimes even destroys them.

Have you ever loaned something to someone who failed to return it to you?

How do you feel when this happens? What do you do?

Have you ever had a person use something of yours who . . .

> misused,
> lost it,
> damaged it, or
> destroyed it?

How do you feel when someone does one of these things to something you own? What do you do?

No one likes to have his or her things misused, lost, damaged, or destroyed.

Everyone likes to have his or her things treated with respect.

If you want other people to respect your things, you will need to make sure that you respect their things.

Remember these two things.

Return the things you borrow from other people.

Try not to misuse, lose, damage, or destroy anyone else's things.

Conclusion

Kindness and respect . . .

that is what GOOD MANNERS are all about.

If you have good manners, you will . . .

>treat other people with kindness and respect,
>and you will

>respect other people's possessions.

If you have good manners, you will follow the golden rule
and treat other people the way you want them to treat you.